Map Tools Help Us Move from Place to Place

Wayan James

Rosen REAL READERS

Rosen Classroom™
New York

My family and I are going on vacation! We are going to Colorado. We are going camping in the Rocky Mountains.

Our car has **GPS** (Global Positioning System). GPS is a virtual map. It gives directions on how to get places. We use it so we know where to go.

There is a **satellite** in outer space. It takes pictures of Earth and makes a computerized map. The map is shown on the GPS screen.

My dad types our starting point into the GPS. Our starting point is home. We live in Wyoming. Wyoming is north of Colorado.

My dad also types our **destination** in the GPS. The GPS has several map tools. It tells us how far away our destination is. It also tells us the best route to take.

My dad starts to drive. We are on our way! My dad uses map tools on the GPS to help us move from place to place.

My dad cannot look at the GPS while he drives. That is unsafe. He turns up the volume on the GPS. A computerized voice tells him the directions.

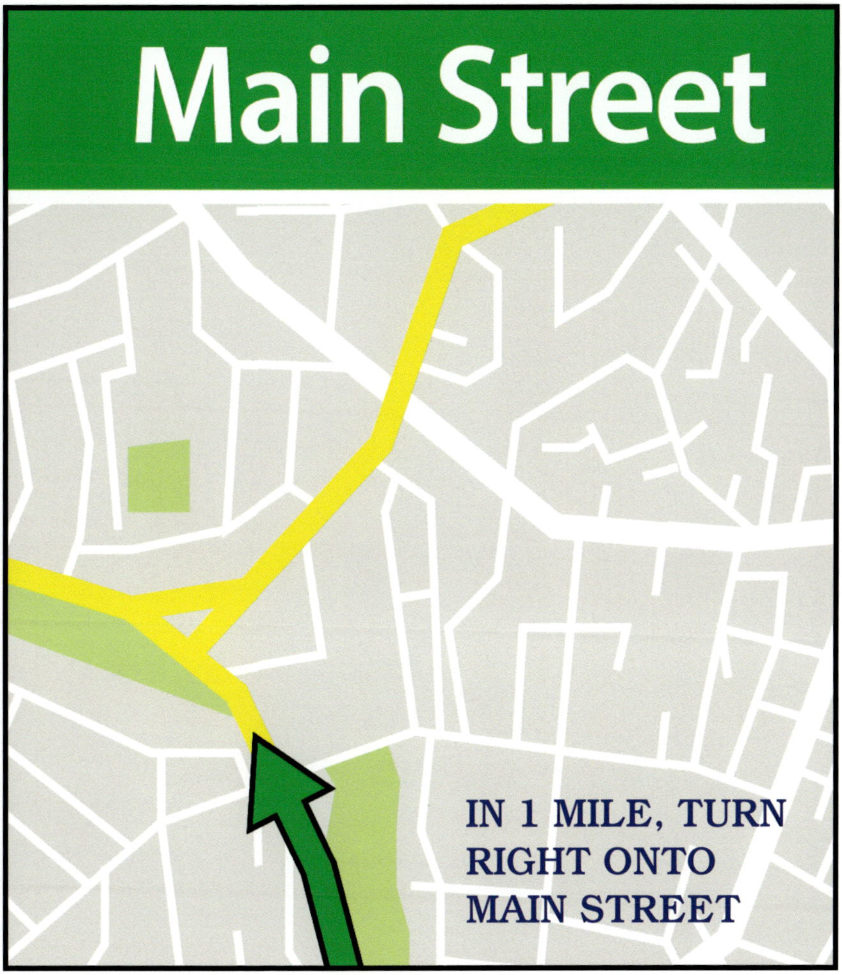

The GPS tells my dad which roads to take. It tells him when a turn is coming. It tells him when to turn, too.

My dad uses the map tools to help us find our way through Denver. Denver is a large city. It is the **capital** of Colorado.

About two hours later, we arrive at Rocky Mountain National Park. The GPS helped us reach our destination!

Glossary

capital The most important city of a country or state.

destination The end point of a trip.

GPS system A navigation system that gives directions.

satellite An object placed in outer space to gather information and take photos of Earth.